MARBLEWORKERS
IN THE
ATHENIAN AGORA

CAROL LAWTON

Agora color photographs by Craig A. Mauzy

AMERICAN SCHOOL OF CLASSICAL STUDIES AT ATHENS
2006

1. A Triton from the second phase of the facade of the Roman Odeion, ca. A.D. 150–175, illustrates the continuity of sculptural practice in the Agora. The torso of the Triton was strongly influenced by one of the figures in the east pediment of the 5th-century B.C. Parthenon. The Triton was later reused in the 5th-century A.D. structure that occupied the site of the Odeion, probably a gymnasium.

Introduction

As early as the 5th century B.C. the poet Pindar in a dithyramb (Fragment 75, line 5) called the Athenian Agora "glorious, richly decorated," and so it was, the setting for justly famous works of art, many of them sculpted from marble. Its buildings had marble decoration and housed dedications in the form of marble statues and reliefs. Its northwestern corner was crowded with marble herms and cavalry dedications on sculpted marble bases. In the Roman period the Agora and its neighborhood were dotted with marble portraits of emperors and other members of the imperial family, philosophers, magistrates, priests, and victorious athletes. Coveted Greek "antique" sculpture as well as contemporary portraits were displayed in private houses on the slopes near the square. The finds from the Agora excavations (1) demonstrate that generations of marbleworkers, many of them working in and around the Agora, made Athens an important center for the production of marble sculpture until its sack by the Herulians in A.D. 267.

2. The gallery of the Stoa of Attalos, displaying sculpture from the Agora excavations

Marbleworkers and the Agora Excavations

ALTOGETHER THE AGORA EXCAVATIONS have uncovered over 3,500 pieces of stone sculpture, which are displayed in the Agora Museum in the Stoa of Attalos or housed in its storerooms (2). Literary and epigraphical evidence tells us that there were statues in and around the Agora by a number of famous Athenian marble sculptors. Almost nothing remains of their originals today, but the excavations have brought to light traces and echoes of their work in the form of statue bases, copies, and adaptations of their famous statues. The excavations have also discovered bases signed by otherwise unknown sculptors and abundant work by the "anonymous" sculptors of architectural decoration, statuettes, and reliefs who usually did not sign their work. In addition to sculpture, marble weights, sundials, furniture parts, and an assortment of kitchen utensils have been found, reminders that marbleworkers produced objects for commercial and household use in addition to those we regard today as art. At the same time, the excavations have revealed the remains of numerous marbleworking establishments in the Agora and its vicinity, as well as a large number of unfinished marble statues, statuettes, reliefs, and utilitarian objects which must have been worked there. Together these sources provide us with an appreciation of the full range of activity of marbleworkers in the Agora.

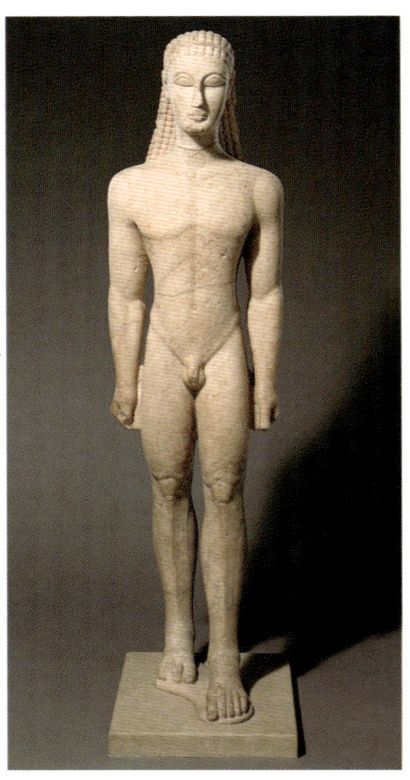 

3. A kouros, from Attica, ca. 600 B.C. (New York, The Metropolitan Museum of Art, Fletcher Fund, 1932, 32.11.1. Photograph © 1997 The Metropolitan Museum of Art)

4. Egyptian statue of Khonsuiraa, early 7th century B.C. (Boston, Museum of Fine Arts, James Fund and Contribution, 07.494. Photograph © 2005 Museum of Fine Arts, Boston)

Marble Sculpture in Greece

IT WAS PROBABLY IN THE SECOND HALF of the 7th century B.C. that Greek sculptors, who had previously carved small statues from wood and their own local limestone, were inspired by contacts with Egypt to carve large-scale statues from a hard stone such as marble. The Egyptians themselves preferred even harder stones such as basalt or granite, but the Greeks quickly developed a preference for their own crystalline white marbles. For most of the Archaic period (ca. 650–480 B.C.) Greek sculptors used marbles imported from the Cycladic islands, but Athenian sculptors occasionally used their own local marbles from two nearby mountains, Penteli and Hymettos, and began to do so on a much larger scale when the quarries of Penteli began to be exploited for building stone early in the Classical period (480–323 B.C.). The Greeks appear to have been influenced initially by Egyptian sculptural techniques and systems of proportions for the human body, and the earliest Greek marble sculptures, such as the freestanding male type called the kouros, bear a superficial resemblance to Egyptian statues (3, 4). But even such an early kouros as the statue in the Metropolitan Museum of Art shows that Greek sculptors had already assimilated the lessons of the Egyptians and had begun working in their own fashion, liberating the figure's limbs from the solid block of stone and analyzing and idealizing the nude body by organizing it into patterns.

5. Seated deities on the east frieze of the Hephaisteion, the well-preserved Classical temple on Kolonos Agoraios, the hill overlooking the Agora, ca. 430–425 B.C.

In the course of the 7th century B.C. the Greeks began building stone temples and decorating them with sculpture, at first made of limestone but by the middle of the Archaic period primarily of marble. In these works, as in the freestanding statues, the figures became more naturalistic as the artists became interested in narrative, making the figures appear more lifelike (5). While very little physical evidence of paint survives today, literary sources and traces of color on newly excavated sculpture indicate that all Greek marble sculpture was originally brightly painted.

Literary evidence and the technical details of surviving statue bases indicate that in the 5th century B.C. marble was overtaken by bronze as the preferred medium for freestanding statues, but Greek sculptors continued to use marble for their architectural sculpture and for grave and votive reliefs. The 4th century brought a renewed interest in marble, with many famous and versatile sculptors working in both marble and bronze. In the Hellenistic period (323–31 B.C.) marble sculptors expanded their range of subjects to meet the demands of a diverse clientele, including Romans, who began to conquer Greek city-states in the 2nd century B.C. The Roman demand for copies and adaptations of all types of sculpture once again made marble the primary medium for sculpture, both for copies and for contemporary originals.

6. Athena Ergane in the workshop of a marble sculptor. Attic red-figure cup by the Foundry Painter, ca. 480 B.C. (Munich, Staatliche Antikensammlung und Glyptothek 2650)

7. Relief depicting Athena Ergane overseeing five female figures. Early 4th century B.C. (S 2495)

ATHENA ERGANE, PATRONESS OF MARBLEWORKERS

IN THE ARCHAIC PERIOD ATHENS became increasingly prosperous and a major center for marble sculpture, attracting artists from all over the Greek world. The initial focus of their work was the Acropolis and its sanctuary of the city's patron deity, Athena. She was worshipped there under a number of names that described her special areas of influence; one of these, Athena Ergane (Athena the Worker), indicates a special relationship between the goddess and the city's artists. Athena Ergane became the patroness of marble- and bronzeworkers, potters, and weavers. Pausanias, author of a 2nd-century A.D. guidebook to Greece, says that the Athenians were the first to worship this aspect of the goddess. The height of her popularity in Athens was the 4th century B.C., when dedications to her were set up on the Acropolis, but she had been depicted much earlier on painted ceramic ware, shown observing the activities of artisans in their workshops (6).

An unusual relief found in the Agora shows Athena Ergane supervising five figures, probably Nymphs, engaged in stoneworking (7). The relief is broken off where an inscription might have explained the scene, but it would have been appropriate decoration for a building decree, perhaps for a fountainhouse since the Nymphs were above all associated with water. Although the figures have been deliberately defaced, the main outlines of the scene are still clear. Athena, wearing her crested helmet, props her foot on a stone and thoughtfully rests her chin on her left hand. She gazes at a figure seated on a low block in front of her, drawing on the ground with a pick hammer and gesturing as she speaks to Athena. Behind her stands a figure apparently taking a measurement, with her right hand stretched high in the air, her left hand held at waist level. The two figures next to her are moving a large block with a lever and fulcrum, while at the far right a figure scrutinizes something held in her right hand, perhaps a tablet with building specifications or a plan.

8. Plan of the Agora showing the location of sculptors' workshops in the residential and industrial area southwest of the Agora, in shops just outside the southeastern corner of the Agora, in the South Square, and in the Library of Pantainos

Marbleworkers' Workshops
in and around the Agora

EXCAVATIONS HAVE DEMONSTRATED THAT marbleworkers were active in the Agora and its vicinity throughout most of its history (8). The earliest sculptors' workshops in the area, established in the early 5th century B.C. and active until destruction by Herulian invaders in the 3rd century A.D., were located in a residential and industrial area southwest of the Agora, in the valley between the Areopagos and the Hill of the Nymphs. Workshops in operation from the 4th century B.C. to the Roman period have also been found just outside the southeastern corner of the Agora. After the sack by the Roman general Sulla in 86 B.C. that damaged most of the buildings in the South Square, sculptors established themselves there in the ruins of the public buildings, occupying them until the area was rehabilitated for public use in the middle of the 2nd century A.D. Sculptors set up shop in two rooms of the western stoa of the Library of Pantainos in the 1st century A.D. and occupied it until the Herulian destruction.

THE WORKSHOPS IN THE RESIDENTIAL AND INDUSTRIAL DISTRICT

The earliest area used by sculptors, the residential and industrial district southwest of the Agora, had sculptors' workshops located along and around a street where so many traces of marble dust and chips were found that the excavators dubbed it the Street of the Marbleworkers. Here rambling mudbrick houses, with rooms clustered around open courtyards, served as both residences and workshops of craftsmen, not only marbleworkers but also bronzeworkers, blacksmiths, and modelers of terracotta statuettes. The courtyards seem to have served as the main working areas; their floors were heaped with marble dust and chips. A small unfinished head of Cycladic marble found in the Street of the Marbleworkers was probably intended to be a kouros statuette and suggests that there were sculptors working in this area as early as the Archaic period (9). Fragments of unfinished marble basins and sandstone finishing stones, identical to those used by modern marbleworkers, came from establishments of the Roman period (10).

9. Unfinished head of a kouros statuette, found in the Street of the Marbleworkers, late 6th or early 5th century (S 1185)

10. An abrasive tool used for finishing sculpture, found in the debris of a sculptor's workshop of the Roman period (ST 456)

The Herm-Carvers in the Residential and Industrial District

Among the fragments of sculpture found in the residential and industrial district are rectangular blocks that served as truncated "arms" for miniature herms (11); their contexts indicate that they were made in the Classical period. A herm is a characteristic Athenian representation of the god Hermes consisting of a head of the god set upon a "body" in the form of a rectangular shaft with no other features than genitals and sometimes these rectangular, truncated "arms" (12). According to literary sources, herms were used to mark gates and doorways. So many of them were set up in the northwestern corner of the Agora, its principal entrance from the port of Piraeus, that the area became known as "the Herms" (13, 14).

The Roman author Plutarch records an anecdote concerning the philosopher Socrates in which he identifies a district of Athens, probably in the residential and industrial district, as the herm-carvers' quarter:

11. An "arm" of a miniature herm from the residential and industrial area southwest of the Agora, 4th century B.C. (S 1426)

12. A group of herms on a fragmentary red-figure pelike by the Pan Painter, ca. 370 B.C. (Paris, Musée du Louvre Cp 10793. Courtesy Réunion des Musées Nationaux/Art Resource, NY)

13. The head of a marble herm found in the area known as "the Herms," ca. 500 B.C. (S 3347)

14. A sculptor carving a herm. Tondo of a red-figure cup by Epiktetos, ca. 520–510 B.C. (Copenhagen, Nationalmuseet CHR. VIII 967)

> Once I was present . . . when Socrates was walking up toward the Symbolon and the house of Andokides. . . . Then he turned and went along the road through the cabinetmakers' quarter, and called out to the friends who had already gone onward to return. . . . Most turned back with him, but certain young men went straight on . . . and as they went through the herm-carvers' quarter, past the law courts, they were met by a herd of pigs, covered with filth and jostling one another.
>
> (Plutarch, *On the Sign of Socrates*, 10.580d–f)

It seems likely that Socrates and his companions were walking toward the Agora from the residential and industrial district. Socrates would have known this district well because his father was a sculptor, and there is a tradition that Socrates himself had been a marbleworker in his youth.

THE WORKSHOP OF MIKION AND MENON

One small house at the edge of the residential and industrial district, on the way into the Agora, was continuously occupied by sculptors from about 475 to 275 B.C., serving both as their residence and workshop (**15**). The first owner, Mikion, inscribed his name on a bone stylus found on the lowest floor of the house (**16**). The last owner, Menon,

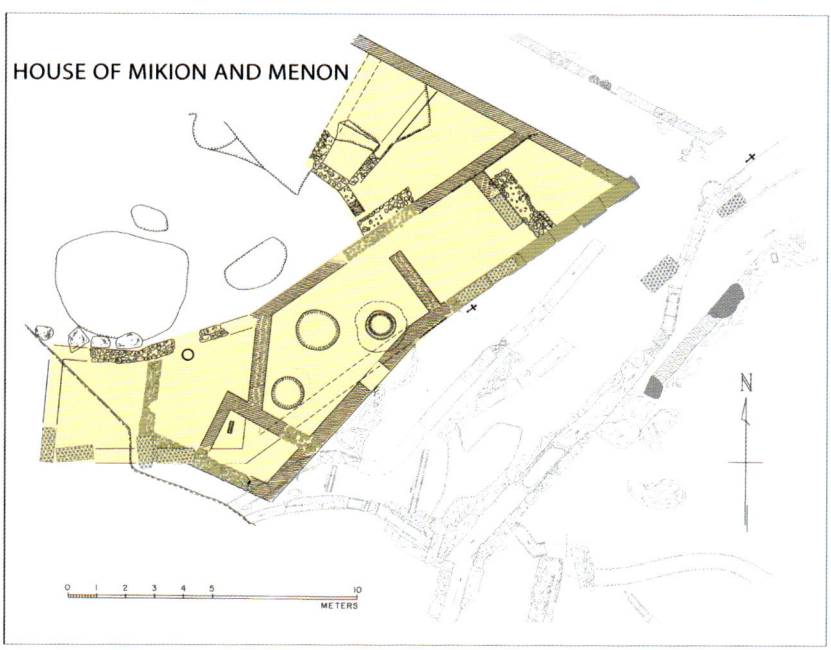

15. Plan of the house of the sculptors Mikion and Menon, in the residential and industrial district southwest of the Agora, 5th–3rd centuries B.C.

16. A bone stylus inscribed with the name of the sculptor Mikion (BI 819)

scratched his name or an abbreviation of it on some of his black-glazed dinnerware (**17**). Mikion and Menon are otherwise unknown, two of the many "anonymous" sculptors of reliefs and other minor works who plied their trade in the city. The floors of their workshop were covered with marble dust, chips, and partially worked stones. In one of the cisterns of its courtyard two unfinished pieces of sculpture were found, a roughly delineated relief head in profile and a roughly blocked-out statuette, possibly of the Mother of the Gods (**18, 19**). Both works demonstrate the economy practiced by the sculptors; they were carved on reused fragments of marble basins. The house in the end was destroyed by fire, probably in the civil strife and turmoil that beset Athens in the early 3rd century B.C., and many of its household contents were dumped into one of its cisterns.

17. A kantharos base inscribed with the name of the sculptor Menon (P 897)

18. An unfinished relief, perhaps a trial piece, showing a roughly delineated profile head, from the house of the sculptors Mikion and Menon, 4th century B.C. The head has been outlined with a point and its surface given an initial smoothing with a claw chisel. (S 201)

19. An unfinished statuette of a seated female figure from the house of the sculptors Mikion and Menon, 4th century B.C. The figure is in the early stages of work, with only its general form and seat roughed out with a point. (S 195)

20. A pit filled with emery powder that had been used for polishing stone, in the ruins of a marbleworker's shop

The Workshops in the South Square

After the sack of Athens by the Roman general Sulla in 86 B.C., marbleworkers, along with metalworkers and potters, set up shop in the heavily damaged buildings of the South Square. These marbleworkers, still active there in the early 2nd century A.D., were perhaps attracted by the remains of a marble temple in the square. Telltale deposits of marble chips were discovered here in shops set up among the ruins, and in the South Stoa II and the East Building, small basins in the clay floors were coated with emery powder that was used to polish small marble objects (20). One of these shops specialized in making small basins for household use. A number of unfinished examples that had been broken while being carved were found abandoned in the shop. One of them, carved from a reused stele and on which inscribed letters can still be seen, again demonstrates the frugality of sculptors making use of discarded material (21). In another shop in the East Building, marble was being sawn into thin slabs for flooring or revetment.

21. An unfinished marble basin with inscribed letters indicating that it was being carved from a reused stele (ST 532)

The Workshop in the Library of Pantainos

The Library of Pantainos was built between A.D. 98 and 102 by the Athenian T. Flavius Pantainos (22). The library itself consisted of two main rooms, with three stoas or porticoes occupied by shops wrapped around it. The shops were probably rented out as a source of income for the library. In two rooms of the library's western stoa, facing the Panathenaic Way, a sculptor's workshop was in operation until it was destroyed by the Herulians in A.D. 267. Marble chips and emery polishing basins and several pieces of finished and unfinished sculpture were found in it (23). Many other unfinished works that formed the core of the Late Roman fortification wall in this area probably came from the ruins of this shop and others like it in houses at the southeastern corner of the Agora.

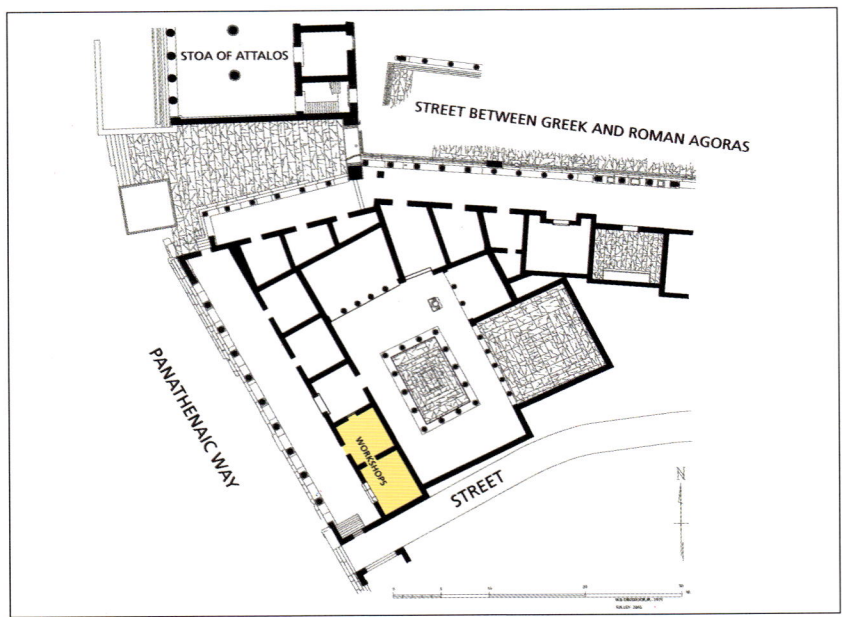

22. Plan of the Library of Pantainos, with a sculptor's workshop in two of its rooms, 2nd–3rd century A.D.

23. Unfinished Roman portrait of a woman, from the Library of Pantainos, ca. A.D. 170. One of the sculptor's measuring points, a tiny hole, is still visible in the middle of the chin. Most of the surface of the face has not yet been smoothed, and the ears, eyebrows, and details of the eyes are not yet finished. The head would have been set into a separately carved body. (S 362)

24. A large unfinished statue of Dionysos still lying in a quarry on Thasos

25. An unfinished statuette of the Mother of the Gods, still showing the preliminary stages of work done with a point (S 957). For a similar, finished Mother of the Gods, see Fig. 39.

Tools and Techniques of Greek and Roman Sculpture

The Quarry

The process of making ancient sculpture began at the quarry. The Athenians were fortunate in having two nearby mountains, Penteli and Hymettos, from which they could extract fine marbles suitable for sculpture. A block of marble was quarried by drilling narrow channels around it, to the desired length, width, and depth of the block. After the block was perforated in this way, it was split away from the marble bed with wedges.

The main outlines of the sculpture could be roughed out in the quarry, in order to minimize the weight of the stone to be transported. A number of very large, unfinished statues abandoned in quarries show that, at least in the Archaic period, the figures might be worked to a fairly advanced state while still in the quarry (**24**).

The Mallet, Point, and Punch

In the first stage of the carving, whether done in the quarry or at the workshop, the preliminary roughing out was done with a wooden or metal mallet and either a pointed iron chisel, an instrument whose cutting edge is a simple point, or an iron punch, a chisel with a squared-off end (**25, 26**).

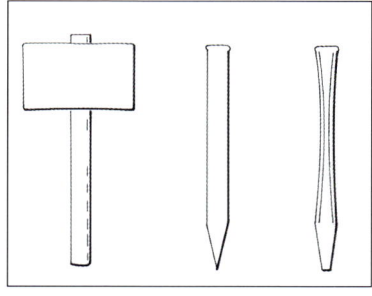

26. Mallet, pointed chisel, and punch

The Chisels

The next stage consisted of the modeling of the figure, and, in reliefs, the smoothing of the sides and background. This work was done with iron chisels, of which there were two main types, the claw or toothed chisel and the flat chisel, of which the round chisel is a variant (27). The claw chisel with a serrated, toothed cutting surface was used for trimming roughly worked surfaces. It leaves a distinctive track formed by the row of its claws. It was used for modeling, between the rough shaping with the point and the finer work with the flat or round chisel. It was also used in the final treatment of wide flat surfaces such as statue bases and the background and sides of reliefs (28). Often the claw marks were left or only slightly smoothed so that they can still be seen beneath the smoothing.

The flat chisel was also used for modeling and for removing a fine layer of stone, for smoothing contours, and for modeling fine, sharp-edged details such as facial features (29). It makes a relatively smooth, ribbon-like surface, with fine lines between the strokes. It is often difficult to see evidence of this tool because when skillfully used it leaves little trace, usually removed in the final smoothing.

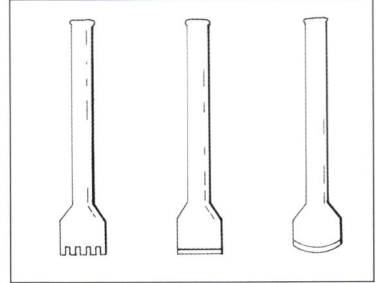

27. Claw chisel, flat chisel, and round chisel

28. A fragment of a relief depicting the god Hermes, with claw-chisel work on the background. Late 5th century B.C. (S 358)

29. An unfinished statuette of Herakles, showing marks of the flat chisel on the body (S 420)

30. Red-figure hydria by the Gallatin Painter showing a carpenter using a bow drill. Ca 490 B.C. (Boston, Museum of Fine Arts, Francis Bartlett Donation of 1912, 13.200. Photograph © 2005 Museum of Fine Arts, Boston)

The Drill

The most versatile tool of marbleworkers was the drill, which was used to form holes, channels, and recesses in all stages of producing sculpture (30, 31). It was used in quarrying, for preliminary shaping, for cutting outlines of relief, for undercutting and hollowing out marble (32), for making channels to separate a figure from its drapery or hair from skin, for making the holes in fine details such as eyes, ears, nostrils, mouths, and curls (33), and for making holes for the attachments of metal ornaments and separately worked marble parts (34), and for repairs (35).

The drill was an instrument with a sharp, usually rounded iron end that was rotated with a strap or bow. It could be used by one man or two, one working the strap or bow, the other guiding the drill itself. The effect of the drill depended upon the angle at which it was applied to the stone. It could be used as a simple drill, making holes at any angle, or it could be used as a "running drill," in which the cutting edge of the drill was held at an angle and moved along the stone while revolving, creating a smooth channel or groove.

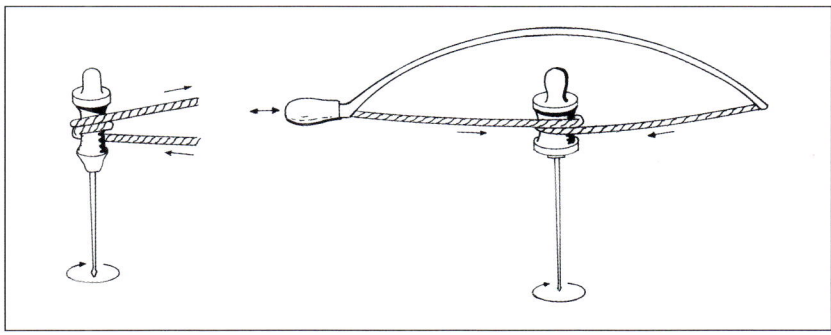

31. Strap and bow drills

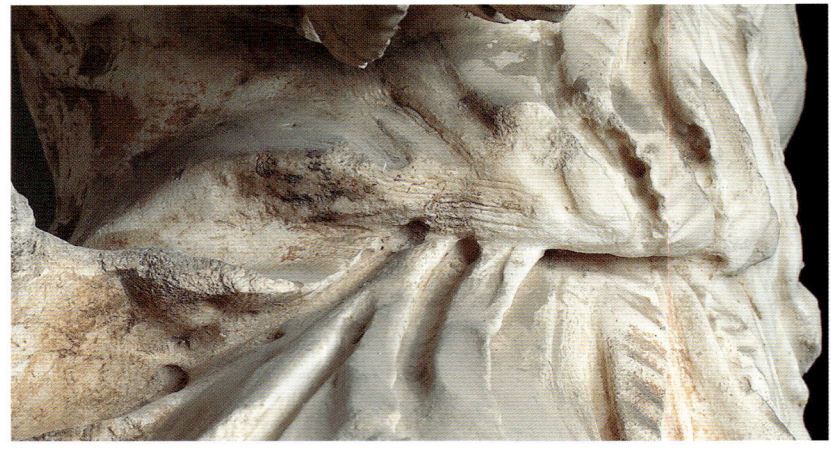

32. Detail of a Nike akroterion (Fig. 49), showing drill marks undercutting the drapery in order to create contrast (S 312)

33. Roman portrait head, with drill holes and channels in the hair, beard, eyes, nostrils, and mouth. 2nd century A.D. (S 2356)

34. A fragment of a torso of Athena with drill holes for attaching bronze snakes to her aegis. Ca. 420 B.C. (S 654)

35. Votive relief to Asklepios and Hygieia, with a drill hole for a repair to the right arm of Asklepios, probably to correct a mistake made by the sculptor. 4th century B.C. (S 2505)

36. Apulian column krater showing a painter coloring the drapery of a statue of Herakles, while on the right the real, less grand Herakles looks on. Ca. 370–360 B.C. (New York, The Metropolitan Museum of Art, Rogers Fund, 1950, 50.11.4. Photograph © 2002 The Metropolitan Museum of Art)

Finishing and Painting

The final stages of work on marble sculpture consisted of smoothing, polishing, and painting. The first stage of finishing the surface of the marble, and sometimes the last, would be accomplished with a rasp, a small-toothed instrument for working away the rough surface left by the previously used tools. If a still smoother finish were desired, especially for the nude parts of the body, the marble would be polished with abrasives such as emery, pumice, or fine sand. The final treatment was the painting, in which pigment was applied in a mixture of hot wax and oil in order to give the surface a luminous quality and to help the color adhere to the marble (36).

Copying

In the Hellenistic and Roman periods, Greek sculptors produced marble copies and adaptations of all types of Greek and Roman sculpture. Although the details of the copying process are not fully known, the technique apparently involved making a plaster cast of an original and transferring measuring points marked on the cast to the piece of marble from which the copy was to be made. The measuring points were frequently applied in a three-point or triangular configuration. Following these points, holes were drilled into the stone and the surplus marble cut away. From these fixed points, and others added as he worked, the sculptor took measurements with calipers to guide his carving. A measuring point on an unfinished work appears as a protuberance with a small depression in its center to hold one point of the calipers.

37. An unfinished head of the "Eubouleus," from the Agora excavations. Roman copy of an original of the 4th century B.C. (S 2089)

38. A finished copy of the "Eubouleus," from Eleusis (Athens, National Museum 181)

The unfinished Roman copy of the "Eubouleus" found in the Agora excavations probably came from one of the sculptors' workshops nearby (37). Its identification as Eubouleus, one of the gods connected with the Eleusinian Mysteries, stems from the discovery of another copy in Eleusis (38), but other identifications, including the youthful Alexander the Great, have been suggested. The Agora copy still has a number of conspicuous measuring points left from the use of triangulation; three of them can be seen on the front, one on the chin and two in the hair just above the forehead.

Famous Marbleworkers in the Agora

LITERARY AND EPIGRAPHICAL EVIDENCE tells us that there were statues in and around the Agora by famous marble sculptors, including works by the 5th-century master Phidias and his associates Agorakritos and Alkamenes, and the 4th-century sculptors Praxiteles, Bryaxis, and Euphranor. Although only one of these original works, a statue by Euphranor, has been identified, excavations have discovered evidence for others in the form of statue bases and copies and adaptations of their work.

Phidias (or Agorakritos?)

Phidias was the most well-known sculptor said to have worked in the Agora. He was the most famous of all Greek sculptors, known not only for his gold and ivory cult statue of Zeus at Olympia, but also for three magnificent, now lost statues on the Athenian Acropolis: his gold and ivory statue of Athena in the Parthenon, a colossal bronze Athena, and the bronze Athena Lemnia. Phidias was also a marbleworker, and according to one ancient account (Plutarch, *Life of Perikles* 13.9) he had a supervisory role in the Periklean building project that included the Parthenon.

Pausanias (1.3.5) says that Phidias was the sculptor of the cult statue of the Mother of the Gods in the Agora, although the Roman author Pliny, in his history of marble sculpture (*Natural History* 36.17), attributes the same statue to Phidias's pupil and associate Agorakritos. Whether the work was by Phidias or Agorakritos, there is considerable evidence from the Agora for the appearance of the statue. Over one

39. Hellenistic statuette of the Mother of the Gods in a naiskos, with a small lion in her lap, a tympanon in her left hand, and small figures of Hermes and Artemis (S 922)

hundred small marble votives to the Mother of the Gods have been found in the Agora excavations, and, while they vary in details, they almost certainly reflect some of the general characteristics of the original statue. Most of them show the Mother enthroned, with a phiale or offering bowl in her right hand, a tympanon or drum in her left, and a lion either beside her or in her lap (**39, 40**).

40. Roman statuette of the Mother of the Gods with a lion at her side. The Mother of the Gods was an Anatolian deity who became identified with the Greek goddesses Rhea and Demeter. (S 731)

41. A well-preserved, simplified version of Alkamenes' Hekate illustrates her three-bodied form. 1st–2nd century A.D. (S 852)

Alkamenes

Another well-known associate of Phidias was Alkamenes, whose most important works in the Agora were the bronze cult statues of Hephaistos and Athena in the Hephaisteion. Alkamenes was also a marbleworker, and works that may be copies or adaptations of two of his most innovative Athenian statues, the triple-bodied Hekate Epipyrgidia and the Hermes Propylaios, have been found in the Agora. Pausanias (2.30.2) points to one of the innovative features of the Hekate: "It was Alkamenes, in my opinion, who first made three images of Hekate attached to one another."

42. Fragment of a herm of the Pergamene type attributed to Alkamenes, from the Agora excavations. 2nd century A.D. (S 1900)

Another new aspect of Alkamenes' triple-bodied Hekate was her style; her flat-footed stance and her drapery, with its stiff, regular folds and wide central fold between the legs, are characteristics of statues of the Archaic period. Alkamenes may have been the first to imitate one or more features of those older works, a style known as archaistic. Approximately 20 archaistic triple-bodied Hekataia have been found in the Agora excavations (41). Hekate was a goddess of the crossroads, and these may have been set up at the crossings of some of the many streets that led to the Agora.

The statue of Hermes Propylaios (Hermes before the Gate) in the form of an archaistic herm is not specifically attributed to Alkamenes by any ancient author, but two Roman herms, one from Pergamon and one from Ephesos, have epigrams attributing them to him. A fragmentary copy of the Pergamene type was found in the Agora excavations (42).

43. The colossal statue of Apollo Patroos, probably by Euphranor, found near the Temple of Apollo Patroos on the west side of the Agora, ca. 330 B.C. (S 2154)

Euphranor

> These pictures [in the Stoa of Zeus] were painted for the Athenians by Euphranor, and he also made the statue of Apollo Patroos in the temple nearby.
>
> Pausanias 1.3.4

The 4th-century sculptor Euphranor was versatile, known as much for his paintings as for his sculpture. A colossal statue of Apollo, found in the early-20th-century Greek excavations in the Metroon next to the Temple of Apollo Patroos on the west side of the Agora, is almost certainly the statue mentioned by Pausanias (**43**). The statue may have been moved to the Metroon after the Agora was sacked by the Herulians. Apollo Patroos (Fatherly Apollo) was worshipped by the Athenians as the father of Ion, the heroic ancestor of the Ionians, who was believed to have settled Attica. The Apollo is depicted as a kithara, or lyre, player. The kithara is almost completely broken away, with just its outline visible along the left side of the statue. Its original position can be seen in a statuette from the Agora that is a rough copy of the original (**44**).

44. Statuette of Apollo Patroos, a copy of the statue of Apollo Patroos by Euphranor, found in a 4th-century A.D. context in a well on Kolonos Agoraios (S 877)

45. Base of a victory monument signed by Bryaxis. Second quarter of the 4th century B.C. (Athens, National Museum 1733)

PRAXITELES AND BRYAXIS

Other famous sculptors are attested in the Agora by the discovery of signed bases of works that are no longer preserved. Two statue bases signed by Praxiteles, one of the most famous sculptors of the 4th century, have been found in the excavations. Not enough of them is preserved, unfortunately, to tell whether the statues were of marble or bronze.

A marble statue base signed and possibly carved by Praxiteles' contemporary Bryaxis was found in the Agora behind the Royal Stoa. Bryaxis was one of four famous sculptors who worked on the Mausoleum of Halikarnassos, one of the seven wonders of the ancient world. The Agora base originally held a bronze tripod commemorating a victory in a cavalry competition. On three sides of the base are reliefs, each depicting a mounted horseman in front of a tripod (45). The fourth side was occupied by the dedicatory inscription naming the victors, and beneath it the artist's signature.

"Anonymous" Sculptors in the Agora

SOME OF THE MOST IMPRESSIVE marble sculpture from the Agora, the architectural sculpture that decorated its temples and stoas, cannot be assigned to known artists (46–49). The designers of the decorative programs were no doubt known in their day, but the carving itself would have been done by a workshop of fairly anonymous marbleworkers. The same was true of the sculptors who worked on the Acropolis. Inscribed building accounts for the Erechtheion name the sculptors who worked on its frieze, none of whom are otherwise known from ancient literature, and their wages, one drachma per day, were the same as those paid other workers on the project.

Some of the most arresting architectural sculptures from the Agora are marble akroteria, statues that stood on the apex or corners of the roof of a building. An akroterion can usually be identified by the weathering on its back, where it was exposed to the elements. The original locations of the akroteria from the Agora are uncertain. They have been attributed to the Hephaisteion, the Temple of Ares, and the Stoa of Zeus.

Others who did not routinely sign their works were the sculptors of smaller sculptures such as statuettes (50) and votive reliefs (51), hundreds of which have been found in the Agora excavations, as well as document reliefs on public inscriptions (52), some of which were set up in the Agora.

46. View of the west frieze of the Hephaisteion, in situ, ca. 430–425 B.C. (A. Frantz)

47. Detail of the west frieze of the Hephaisteion: Centaurs pounding Kaineus into the ground (A. Frantz)

48. An akroterion perhaps depicting a Nereid that has been attributed to the Hephaisteion. Late 5th century B.C. (S 182)

49. A statue of Nike, an akroterion that has been attributed to the Temple of Ares or the Stoa of Zeus. Early 4th century B.C. (S 312)

50. A Hellenistic statuette of Aphrodite, with the baby Eros behind her right shoulder. The statuette is a rare example of sculpture from the Agora with some of its paint still preserved. (S 1192)

51. A votive relief depicting Demeter, her daughter Persephone, Eubouleus with the baby Ploutos, and worshippers. Demeter, the goddess of agriculture, was one of the most important deities worshipped in the vicinity of the Agora. 4th century B.C. (S 1251)

52. Sculptors sometimes worked with masons to produce reliefs on inscribed public documents. This relief on the anti-tyranny law of 337/6 B.C. depicts Democracy crowning Demos (the Athenian People). (I 6524)

Omega House and the End of Marble Sculpture in the Agora

A LARGE AND SUMPTUOUSLY DECORATED Late Roman house excavated just outside the Agora on the north slope of the Areopagos once held a large and diverse collection of sculpture of high quality dating from the 4th century B.C. to the 3rd century A.D. Named Omega House after the section of the excavation in which it is located, the house was built in the 4th century A.D. and may have functioned as a philosophical school. Some time in the first half of the 6th century its sculpture was discarded, either reused as building material during the final occupation of the house or thrown into its wells (53–58). Three pieces representing pagan deities were deliberately defaced (53–55). Lamps decorated with crosses and other finds associated with the final phase of Omega House suggest that it was being used by Christians, most likely those who destroyed the fine collection of sculpture. The Christian emperor Julian closed the pagan philosophical schools in A.D. 529.

The collection of Omega House included statues, reliefs, and portrait heads, many probably disturbed from their original locations by the violence of the Herulian invasion of A.D. 267 and acquired as "antiques" by the original owner of the house. The collection demonstrates that even after the Herulian destruction of the Athenian marbleworking establishments, wealthy Romans appreciated and collected Athenian sculpture from the Classical period onward, and it was only the arrival of Christianity that finally erased most traces of the marbleworkers of the Athenian Agora.

53. Votive relief depicting Hermes handing over the infant Dionysos to the Nymphs, dedicated ca. 330 B.C. and reused in Omega House. All of the figures have been defaced. (I 7154)

54. Relief depicting Artemis, found in a well of Omega House. Her face has been mutilated. 2nd–3rd century A.D. (S 2361)

55. Decapitated statue of Athena, found reused as a doorstep in Omega House. 2nd century A.D. (S 2337)

56. Head of the goddess Nike, found in a well of Omega House. 2nd century A.D. (S 2354)

57. Bust of the emperor Antoninus Pius (A.D. 138–161), found in a well of Omega House (S 2436)

58. Portrait bust of a Roman matron, found in a well of Omega House. 3rd century A.D. (S 2435)